All About Scabs

By Genichiro Yagyu

Translated by Amanda Mayer Stinchecum

A CURIOUS NELL BOOK

KM Kane/Miller Book Publishers

Brooklyn, New York & La Jolla, California

I wonder if I can pick off this scab? I wonder if I can? I really want to.

DON'T
PICK
THAT
SCAB!!

You really shouldn't pick scabs.

Why not? Scabs itch. When you touch them, they feel rough.
It just makes you want to pick at them.

I think it's okay
to pick *this* kind
of scab.

Eeek!
Are you sure?

Have you ever had a scab?

Once, when I
skinned my knee,
it made a scab.

When I picked
off the scab, blood
started dripping out.
It was scary.

Look, I have a scab on
my knee right now.

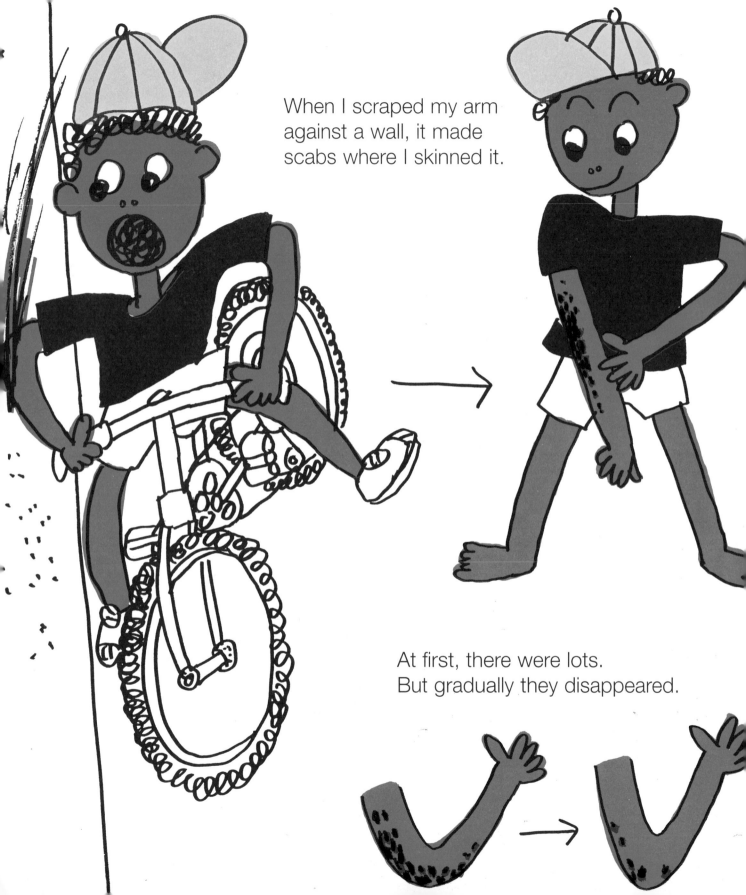

When I scraped my arm against a wall, it made scabs where I skinned it.

At first, there were lots.
But gradually they disappeared.

After my shoe rubbed against
my heel, it made a scab.

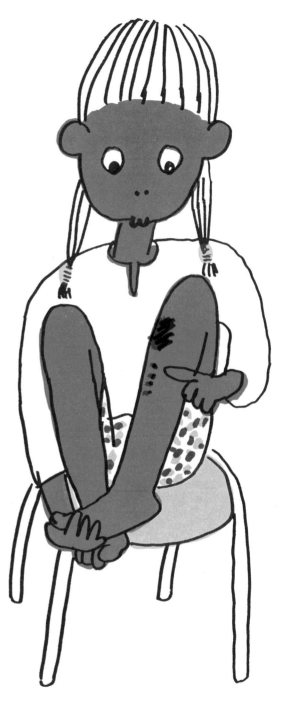

Here are *my* scabs. One big
one and four little ones.

When I fell down and skinned my face, it made scabs next to my eye and below my ear. I even had a few *on* my ear.

When I scraped the skin under my nose, it made *this* kind of scab! AARGH!

What is a scab actually made of?

Is it hardened blood?

Is it some waste material the body
is trying to get rid of?

I say a scab is a lump of flesh.
Because it's flesh you pick at, it's "pick-flesh"!
(Get it? "Pig-flesh"!)

Since the scab forms where the skin bleeds, maybe a scab is just blood after all?

My scab is paper thin. Could it be paper?

Maybe a scab is made of something like poop that comes out of a sore. It's the poop of a sore!

Oh, you say everything is poop!

My scab is hard and thick, like a cookie.

Wonder if I could eat it?

I once ate a scab. YUCK!

A scab <u>is</u> made of blood. It's hardened blood.

That's why it's reddish in color.

Blood doesn't clot when it's circulating inside your body. But when you hurt yourself and it bleeds, that blood tends to harden.

Plasma and fibrin in your blood gather at the surface of a wound. They thicken the blood there and make it hard.

Oh! It stopped bleeding.

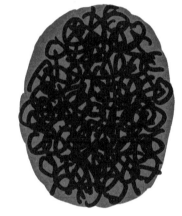

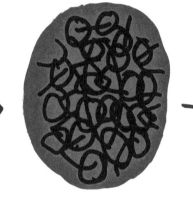

The wound bleeds.	Plasma and fibrin clump together.	As they increase, the blood gets sticky.	Plasma and fibrin cells stick together, and the blood gets thick and hardens.

Here, plasma and fibrin cells are drawn very large to make them easy to see. Actually, if you lined up 1,000 cells side by side, they would only be about this big – .

When your blood thickens and gets hard, it makes a kind of cover on the wound, so that your blood can no longer run out. This lid of hardened blood that forms over the wound is the scab.

What happens underneath a scab?

Once I did look under a scab.
There were red, yellow and white spots.
And the flesh looked very raw.
IT WAS SCAREEEE.

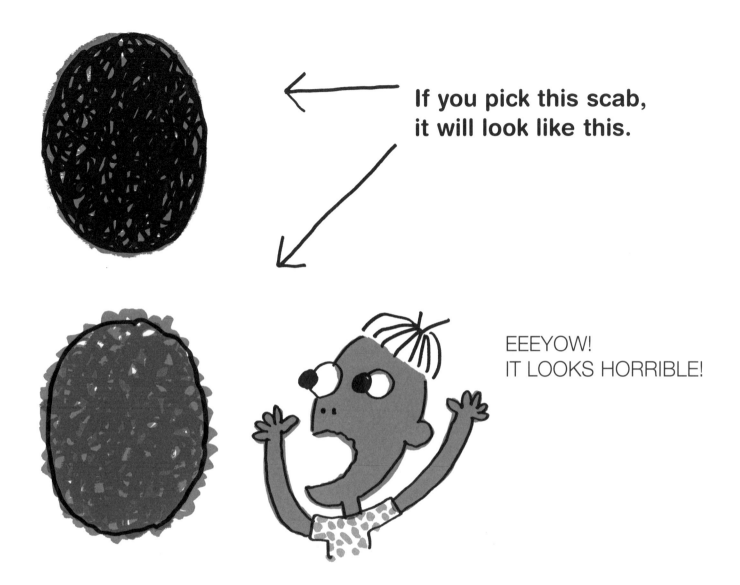

If you pick this scab, it will look like this.

EEEYOW!
IT LOOKS HORRIBLE!

In the "horrible" place under the scab, new skin is quickly forming. But until it's completely formed, the scab stays in place.

If we magnify the skin that covers our bodies, it will look sort of like this drawing.

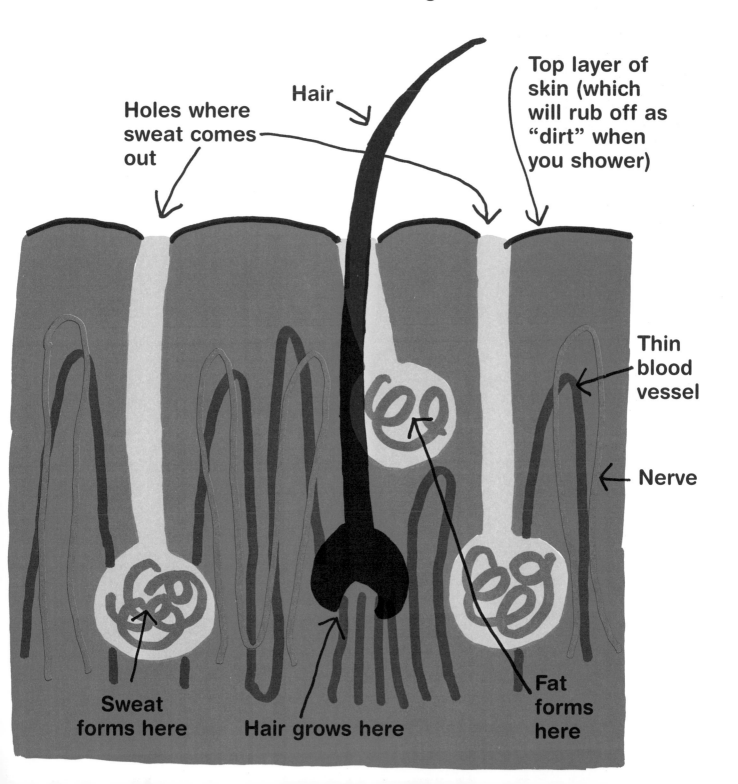

Holes where sweat comes out

Hair

Top layer of skin (which will rub off as "dirt" when you shower)

Thin blood vessel

Nerve

Sweat forms here

Hair grows here

Fat forms here

In the skin are places where sweat and hair are formed. Also, the skin is full of nerves that feel "it's hot," or "it's cold," or "it hurts" and so on. And our skin is teeming with tiny blood vessels, called capillaries, through which the blood circulates.

The very top layer of the skin is a little tough. It keeps germs from getting in.

I know there are holes here where sweat comes out. But I can't see any holes...

The skin works very hard to keep germs like us from getting inside the body. Too bad! BUT when the skin breaks, WE'LL GET IN!

Skin

Aaaaah!

It's bleeding where I scraped
my knee.
The skin's broken. Oh no!
NOW GERMS CAN GET IN!

There's nothing to worry about. This kind of scratch will stop bleeding in just a little while. The hardened blood will form a scab and keep the germs out.

Make sure to rinse off any mud or dirt around the wound.

The skin is broken where it's scraped.

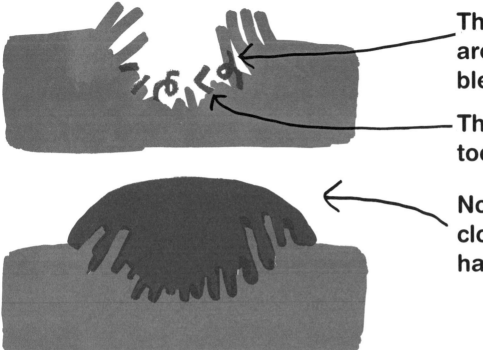

The blood vessels are broken, so it's bleeding.

The nerves are split too, so it hurts.

Now the blood is clotting, and a scab has begun to form.

Finally, the scab completely covers the wound.

continued . . .

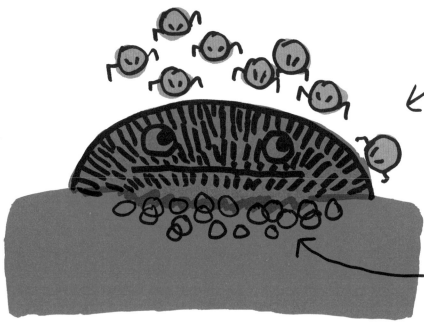

The scab keeps germs from getting into the wound.

White blood corpuscles have gathered around too. They are part of your blood. Their job is to fight germs.

Now that the scab has completely covered the wound, new skin forms beneath it very quickly.

The scab's work is done.

At a certain point, the scab will fall off naturally.

Five days ago I skinned my knee. New skin must have already formed under the scab. It looks like it's almost ready to fall off. But not quite.

Just a little longer

NOW UNDER CONSTRUCTION

HEY!

The scab's gone.

It must have
fallen off
without my
knowing it.

The place where the scab fell off is pink and smooth, a little puffy and swollen. And it feels weird.

Gee! I miss my scab.

Maybe I'll get another one soon . . .